CHRISTIAN WIMAN

ONCE IN THE WEST

Christian Wiman is the author of seven books, including a memoir, *My Bright Abyss: Meditation of a Modern Believer* (FSG, 2013); *Every Riven Thing* (FSG, 2010), winner of the Ambassador Book Award in poetry; and *Stolen Air: Selected Poems of Osip Mandelstam.* He currently teaches religion and literature at the Yale Institute of Sacred Music and Yale Divinity School.

ONCE

IN THE

WEST

ONCE

IN THE

WEST

CHRISTIAN WIMAN

FARRAR, STRAUS AND GIROUX

NEW YORK

FARRAR, STRAUS AND GIROUX
18 West 18th Street, New York 10011

The Library of Congress has cataloged the hardcover edition as follows:
Wiman, Christian, 1966–
    [Poems. Selections]
    Once in the West / Christian Wiman. — First edition
      pages   cm
    ISBN 978-0-374-22701-2 (hardcover)
    I. Title

PS3573.I47843 O63 2014
811'.54—dc23

                                          2014000389

Paperback ISBN: 978-0-374-53570-4

Designed by Gretchen Achilles

Our books may be purchased for promotional, educational, or business use.
Please contact your local bookseller or the Macmillan Corporate and
Premium Sales Department at 1-800-221-7945, extension 5442,
or by e-mail at MacmillanSpecialMarkets@macmillan.com.

www.fsgbooks.com
www.twitter.com/fsgbooks • www.facebook.com/fsgbooks

1   3   5   7   9   10   8   6   4   2

For Martin Jean and Peter Hawkins

CONTENTS

THREE: MORE LIKE THE STARS

PRAYER

For all
the pain

passed down
the genes

or latent
in the very grain

of being;
for the lordless

mornings,
the smear

of spirit
words intuit

and inter;
for all

the nightfall
neverness

inking
into me

even now,
my prayer

is that a mind
blurred

by anxiety
or despair

might find
here

a trace
of peace.

ONE

═══════════════════

SUNGONE
NOON

Mad sand
and the sungone noon

stinging me
back to me

my mind fields
my hands shields . . .

BACK

Goof the noon
no one knows

back of the house
back of the shed

back of God
with his everair

assurances
and iron

injunctions:
sing a little nonce

curse
for the curse

of consciousness
coming on you

like a rash:
little boy

lifting
little mountains

from the trash
to stare down

the angry
eons

in the oil eyes
of the horny toad.

Goof the noon
gone too soon

like the house
and shed,

like the boy
in whom you sit,

your back
to the back

of the old
commode,

where a few flowers
flower

out of all the years
of shit.

TELL ME

If the courts
are asphalt

and the nets
chain-link;

if it's a herculean
feat

to fuck unseen
at the Sonic;

if a slick
piglet

leaps
from a child's yelp

amid a roar
of beer

and such ugly
incorrigibles

as Clack and Skoot,
Messrs. Butt

and Derryberry
chalk their scores

and hawk
their spit

all afternoon
in the laughteryawn

of the bull-
smelling stalls;

if, as the sky
grains again

and the ground's
in every mouth,

someone homeward
turns

a pick-up
aboil

with birddogs
and someone skyward

syrups
Durn . . .

tell me:

can it be
tragedy?

BIG COUNTRY

One answer's
cancer
on a slow boil
in the bones
of a woman
who sleeps
five feet
from the wide-screen
rape-screams
of a woman
her granddaughter,
motherless,
fourteen,
mainlines.

It's Christmas
in Abilene,
baked shanks
and blackeyes
cloying
the double-wide,
kerosene splashing
over an actor
acting terrified
of death.

Enter the pug.
It sniffs
the rinsed
vomit tub,
halfheartedly humps
Uncle Brunson's
un-broken-in
boot, spills in
and out of Ora's
happily distracted
hands, then
quicklicks
awake the raving
raging woman
he was bought
from the mall
to mollify.

Enter the woman
into the woman
raving
raging
at the pug
ogred
over her,
razormusic,
and the smell
of something
burning.

NATIVE

At sixteen,
sixteen miles

from Abilene
(Trent,

to be exact),
hellbent

on being not
this, not that,

I drove
a steamroller

smack-dab over
a fat black snake.

Up surged a cheer
from men

so cheerless
cheers

were grunts, squints,
whisker twitches

it would take
a lunatic acuity

to see.
I saw

the fat black snake
smashed flat

as the asphalt
flattening

under all ten tons
of me,

flat as the landscape
I could see

no end of,
flat as the affect

of distant killing
vigilance

it would take a native
to know was love.

CALCULUS

A soul
extrapolated

from the body's
need

needs a body
of loss:

is that, then,
what we were

given
in that back-

seat, sweat-
soaked, skin-

habited heaven
of days

when rapture
was pure

beginning
and sinning

praise?

ONE

One raised goats;
one raced around barrels
(bareback to teach me);

one liked it most
at midnight
on the pole-vaulting mat

(or did she feign that
to reach me?);
one, muddy-buttocked,

chigger-bit, bit me.
Tank-topped I rode
the rock-n-roll

of my T-topped Trans-Am
down the drag
of that drag town

in which, I'm told,
one raised four children
on her own; one fiended

wine; one roused
her roustabout boyfriend
from her best friend's

bed; and one,
who laughing slapping
leapt up nude as dawn,

her backside
fossiled in the lakeside,
died.

KEYNOTE

I had a dream of Elks,
antlerless but arousable all the same,

before whom I proclaimed the Void
and its paradoxical intoxicating joy,

infinities of fields our very natures
commanded us to cross,

the Sisyphean satisfaction of a landscape
adequate to loss—

and as I spoke inspired
farther and farther afield from my notes

I saw James Wesson whiten
to intact ash

big-boned Joe Sloane shrivelcrippled
tight as tumbleweed

I saw wren-souled Mary Flynn die again
in Buzz's eyes

I saw
I saw

like a huge claw
time tear

through the iron
armory and the baseball fields

the slush-puppy stand
the little pier at Towle Park Pond

until I stood strangered
before the living staring Godfearing men

who knew me when.

RUST

Mamie Thrailkill, 1894–1990

A hammer a father's forever behind
or a Dust Bowl woodpecker high in pines?

Blue purl and milkfeel of a child taking shape,
or child-sized tumor taking over?

She sits in the timestorm time's turned into,
shinedying in her easy chair.

Love is there:

handmade houseshoes and a cairn of yarn;
a Bible thumbed to nearly nothing;

the percolator's way of holding and withholding
every inmost stare and state.

And hate:

purple-kerchiefed, stupid-toothed, a Stuckey's Aunt Jemima
stalls her grin above a red cut of melon;

on the sideboard a lean late husband
hatchets through a half-dozen grainy days.

Shy birdbride, fourteen, all night you hide
under the bed divining sighs, each
                              iron
                                    squeak.

Sweet Christ! how much itch and last sass
must a middle-aged man with one mean mule

and a patch of pissed-on dirt endure?
Not much, not much.

Is nothing pure?
Is it the soul's treason to think so?

Is it nature's to wink so
on the birdhouse hinges and the chain-links

until the brain breaks
upon a paingleaned God

too meaningful
to mean?

I just went to bed, she said
of her son's sons' deaths just days apart

from slapcheek,
from brain fever,

from the virus
of us.

And art?

When the rocking stops.
A sense of being henceforth always after.

A hungry angry mule crying its dumb ton
of rust.

LESS

Silas,
say less

than silence.
In a dawn

lost to all
but me,

be,
Silas, beyond

the hay bale
harboring

kittens
no one now

has the heart
to kill;

and touching
nothing

touch
my head

so we can be alive
together,

Silas,
as together

we are dead.

MUSIC MAYBE

Too many elegies elevating sadness
to a kind of sad religion:

one wants in the end just once to befriend
one's own loneliness,

to make of the ache of inwardness—

something,
                music maybe,

or even just believing in it,
and summer,

and the long room alone
where the child

chances on a bee
banging against the glass

like an attack of happiness.

BLACK DIAMOND

*For a couple of winters during my childhood my family went
on skiing trips with another family from the small town where
we lived. The youngest child, Jeff, was a daredevil, and he and
I spent our days together and became close. He was seven or so,
I was five or six years older. Several years later, after I had left
town, Jeff climbed to the top of the raftered coliseum, perhaps to
survey the scene below, perhaps to play a joke. In any event he
slipped and fell two hundred feet to his death.*

And ever after rafters would speak to me
of falling:

a child's voice calling
How 'bout a bit a birdseed Birdman?

while the chairlift chugs and jolts us up the snow
of New Mexico

so that downward soundward
we might fly.

Seven years old.

When heaven fears its secrets will be told
it tells them to the least and the lost of us:

Headfirst and howling (so they said)
something that will not stop echoing

in my head, he slips
from the topmost most-banned beam of Snyder Coliseum

downward
soundward

to the lightswirled world that even in my heart
is hard.

There are eyes, there are hands
there are lives so otherlit

so freed of the need to mean
that to elegize is obscene.

Trickster, little broken
jokester,

with your contempt for years
and your disdain for gravity

your highwire haywire feats
your pockets packed with sweets

go
      Birdboy
            go

faster through the snow
faster down the untracked

black

diamond demanding someone
let there be someone
                    winged enough

to catch you.

PREY

The peeled-grape feel of sun before sun:
undawn:

light like a live thing
creeping out of cracks and nooks:

don't move
don't breathe:

this chill attentiveness all men are meant to love:
tight in the blind

feeling
feeling

go out of my hands:
sighting down the sightlines

be still
be still

until the shadows coalesce
into something I can kill.

BLINK

We were all an oily rabble,
some spiritless unguent oozing out of us

more surely than the shine
on our possum noggins.

We were all a cuddle of lean fleas,
bovine sundumb Sunday zombies

chewing chewing our little cuds of God.
Jesus, even the horizon's woozy,

and the pumpjacks, galactically black,
fucking the earth; space

so supremely empty
you could hear

an extinction's
last, baffled

blink.

WE LIVED

We lived in the long intolerable called God.
We seemed happy.

I don't mean content I mean heroin happy,
donkey dentures,

I mean drycleaned deacons expunging suffering
from Calcutta with the cut of their jaws

I mean the always alto and surely anusless angels
divvying up the deviled eggs and jello salad in the after-rapture

I mean
to be mean.

Dear Lord forgive the love I have
for you and your fervent servants.

I have so long sojourned Lord
among the mild ironies and tolerable gods

that what comes first to mind
when I'm of a mind to witness

is muriatic acid
eating through the veins

of one whose pains were so great
she wanted only out, Lord, out.

She too worshipped you.
She too popped her little pill of soul.

Lord if I implore you please just please leave me alone
is that a prayer that's every instant answered?

I remember one Wednesday witness told of a time
his smack-freaked friends lashed him

to the back of a Brahman bull that bucked and shook
until like great bleeding wings the man's collarbones

exploded out of his skin.
Long pause.

"It was then," the man said, "right *then* . . ."
Yes. And how long before that man-

turned-deacon-turned-scourge-of-sin
began his ruinous and (one would guess) Holy Spirit–less
    affair?

At what point did this poem abandon
even the pretense of prayer?

Imagine a man alive in the long intolerable time
made of nothing but rut and rot,

a wormward gaze
even to his days' sudden heavens.

There is the suffering existence answers:
it carves from cheeks and choices the faces

we in fact are;
and there is the suffering of primal silence,

which seeps and drifts like a long fog
that when it lifts

leaves nothing
but the same poor sod.

Dear God—

REST HOME

2011

At the rest home
rest is
precarious:
limbs and times
spasm and
for a time
vanish:
then the little up-
ruptures re-
settling
as of dust
deep in the unhappened
avalanche.

Already not yet
noon
and a line
of squeegied
people
rots and totters,
tilts and mutters
outside the dining
hall. Antbites
of irritation
crawl all over
the attendant's
skin:
will she scream

and fling
them off?
Will the earth
open and God
swallow
this debacle
of animal,
these last
crushed-
cricket
twitches
of existence
testifying
less to survival
than simply
to less?

No.
The doors open
as they always
do, the heart
softens
as it often
does,
and into a dim
Because
limp the loved
and the unloved,
some hungry,
some not,
but each

with a place
they know
today, each
of a mind
to stay.

What voice is this cut in the air
as though a wound itself had speech

Give her small hands
Give her dark hair

Give her a wound no word can reach

AFTER

I got a hitch
in my git-along
she says,
having got along
six decades
and change
without a father,
who got along
passably well
with his irascible will
and rotgut quiet
until,
one night in '52,
while her face
flashed in her knife
and the boys
groaned at okra,
he shot his wife
and himself
too.

I got a hitch,
she says,
who said
nary a word
nearly a year
clenching
like a withered

scripture
a napkin
nearly skin
by the time
they coaxed
her open,

in my git-along,
a little wrong
to right the rift
running
right through
the grain
of things,
like the rat
an undrugged
undressed
husband
whacks at
laughdamning
God, like
the little kiss
and gift
a son
bestows
instead of
himself,
like the kitchen
wall clock
that's ever after
all clocks

saying only
after
after
after:

I got a hitch
in my git-along—
a cactus song
for the twin
infants
unscrunching
out of sleep
to wonder
and coo
at Grandma,
kaleidoscopically
clothed
and grinning
to beat all
git-out,
who lifts
with her hitch
and draws
from her drawl
an almost English
ting:

Here's something!
Once I sat
at the zoo
when your daddy
was just

a little tick
of a thing
like you
and sad
so sad I was
and do you know
what the good Lord
saw fit to give?
Boo!
A pigeon
pooped
upon my head.

SUNDAY SCHOOL

A city of loss lit in me.

Childhood: all the good
Godcoddled children

chiming past
the valley of the shadow:

old pews, old views
of the cotton fields

north, south,
east, west,

foreverness
sifting down like dust

when —
        stabdazzling darkness,
        icequiet:

        towers of glare,
        blacksleek streets,

        everywhere an iron
        eloquence

        and a sense
        of high finish

hived with space
like a face

honed
by a loneliness

it never came
to know.

I came to know it.

MEMORY'S MERCIES

Memory's mercies
mostly aren't

but there were
I swear
      days
veined with grace

like a lucky
rock
     ripping
electrically over

whatever water
there was—

ten skips
       twenty
in the telling:

all the day's aches
eclipsed

and a late sun
belling

even sleeping Leroy
back
        into his body
to smile
at some spirit-lit

tank-rock
skimming the real

so belongingly
no longing
            clung to it
when it plunged

bright as a firefly
into nowhere,

I swear.

EVEN THE DEMON

It takes a real cow
to bite beyond
the prickly pear's
sharp spokes.

It takes a brain
of stone
or canny man
to coax

from thorn and husk
sustaining fruit.
It takes hunger,
it takes thirst

to taste
all the tender
interiors
of hell—

upon which,
it is said,
even the Demon
chokes.

WINTERLUDE

Painlady leaning into pain as every day she does:
this time it's mine, this time my spine's

rivering new forms of formlessness:
lava crawling creaturely through my jaw,

one shoulder shot through with shineless light
only the unliving could see by.

Where am I?

What happened to time (to mind)
that I should turn from the safe dangers of memory

to this burn of unbeing,
this mad metastasis of Now?

Painlady lay upon my tongue the morphine moon,
let your opiate hope

bloom once more in my brain
that I might be blessedly less

alive—

not howling homeward like that hound
(I hear him now)

hellfired tongue to gut
by some country Satan

who'd seasoned meat
with shattered glass.

BELIEVING GREEN

2810 El Paso Street, 1974

Solitary as a mast on a mountaintop,
an ocean of knowing long withdrawn,

she dittied the days, grew fluent in cat,
felt, she said, each seed surreptitiously split

the adamantine dark, believing green.
It was the town's torpor washed me to her door,

it was the itch existence stranded me on that shore
of big-lipped shells pinked with altogether other suns,

random wall-blobs impastoed with jewels and jowls
sometimes a citizen seemed to peek through,

inward and inward all the space and spice
of her edible heavens.

O to feel again within the molded dough
wet pottery, buttery cosmos, brain that has not cooled;

to bring to being an instant
sculpture garden: five flashlit jackrabbits locked in black.

From her I learned the earthworm's exemplary open-mindedness,
its engine of discriminate shit.

From her I learned all the nuances of neverness
that link the gladiola to God.

How gone she must be, graveless maybe,
who felt the best death would be for friends to eat you,

whose last name I never even knew:
dirt-rich mouse-proud lady who Rubied me

into a life so starred and laughtered there was no need
for after.

LOVE'S LAST

Love's last urgency is earth
and grief is all gravity

and the long fall always
back to earliest hours

that exist nowhere
but in one's brain.

From the hard-packed
pile of old-mown grass,

from boredom, from pain,
a boy's random slash

unlocks a dark ardor
of angry bees

that link the trees
and block his way home.

I like to hold him holding me,
mystery mastering fear,

so young, standing unstung
under what survives of sky.

I learned too late how to live.
Child, teach me how to die.

Under the unheavened
sky:
> *over the rocky acres'*

outgrowths
outgrowing

even the dream
> *of water:*

apart from the lone mesquite
> *twisted and*
> *constricted*
like a consternation of nature:

above the yucca's frozen
explosion:

> *one*

tatterdemalion dandelion
adrift in the air

> *like happy ash*

TWO

MY STOP

IS GRAND

MY STOP IS GRAND

I have no illusion
some fusion
    of force and form
will save me,
bewilderment
    of bonelight
ungrave me

as when the El
shooting through a hell
    of ratty alleys
where nothing thrives
but soot
    and the ratlike lives
that have learned to eat it

screechingly peacocked
a grace of sparks
    so far out and above
the fast curve that jostled
and fastened us
    into a single shock of—
I will not call it love

but at least some brief
and no doubt illusionary belief
        that in one surge of brain
we were all seeing
one thing:
        a lone unearned loveliness
struck from an iron pain.

Already it was gone.
Already it was bone,
        the gray sky
and the encroaching skyline
pecked so clean
        by raptor night
I shuddered at the cold gleam

we hurtled toward
like some insentient herd
        plunging underground at Clark
and Division.
And yet all that day
        I had a kind of vision
that's never gone completely away

of immense clear-paned towers
and endlessly expendable hours
        through which I walked
teeming human streets,
filled with a shine
        that was most intimately me
and not mine.

INTERIOR

Flat light and the white aisles of cotton,
sky like an idea of blue.
There's no space like this,
wide, fraught with God.

The past is not a place
but story upon story gone so far
inside of things it takes a touch
of almost inhuman love to tell them.

To be the wire through which that current burns,
conducting the stone's slow accretion
like a cry, deciphering sunlight,
to pluck sound from the rings of a tree . . .

More than this I want the silence that ensues,
to believe in nothing but the fact of absence,
striking out again in my hard horizonless country
whose one road releases me like heat as I walk on.

LITTLE KILLING DITTY

I have forgotten the little killing ditty
whispered to the red birds and the blue birds and the brown birds
not one of which I ever thought to give a name.

In the tall mesquite mistaking our yard
for a spacious place, I plugged away with my pellet gun
and got them often even in the eye, for I was trained

to my craft by primordial boredom
and I suppose some generic, genetic rage
I seem to have learned to quell, or kill.

They dropped like the stones I'd throw in Catclaw Creek
or fluttered spastically and panickedly up
whereupon I took more tenacious aim—

much more difficult now because they moved
—not me, frozen as if in a camera's flash—
troubling the tyranny of the ordinary

as if a wave of meaning or unmeaning
went rippling like heat through the yard.
Fire and fire and they fell and they fall, hard.

I felt nothing, and I will not betray those days
if days are capable of being betrayed,
by pretending a pang in my larval heart

or even some starveling joy when Tuffy yelped.
I took aim at the things I could not name.
And the ditty helped.

WARTIME TRAIN

Bone-men, smoke-souls, river-wraiths,
    I am, I know, no light
        but the light of time
           passing.

These sparks that speak
    departure, that make the cold night
        colder: this cry I am inside
          is not mine.

What use to beat my hands
    against the glass?
        That the past
          might pass?

The instant teems
    meaning,
        and meanness,
          like ants in sweets.

Down the river, darkness embodied
    bobs up and down
        like a ship shaped by a child
          or incompetent god

Or an earth
    so up-ruptured
        even the mountains
            are migratory.

—*after Sándor Csoóri*

PORTRAIT OF AN ARTIST

Even eighty he was upright, vainlean,
flush with thatch like a lucky chickadee;

a kind of sniff-the-fingers juvenescence to him,
something cerulean, otherwhere, a purity

of emptiness you had to admire,
like Phoenix, for instance, Palm Springs,

or some other sunland where mortals go to die.
Not him. How can death touch what life has not,

what night nullify the six-sharp whiskey
ambering in him, the cloud-skirted virgins,

the sundown sandstone tigering up the sky?

RAZING A TOWER

Once in the west I rose to witness
the cleverest devastation.
It was early but I was late
and the quiet into which I crept—

nightshifters, gin-veined men,
a stare with a burn scar and a rosary—
was intimate, inviolate, tribal.
I didn't so much keep it as was kept.

A whisper-rupture, feathery detonation,
last concussive flush of a great heart giving way
and all the outworn stories collapsed
in a kind of apocalyptic plié.

Vanish the dancer and the dance remains
a time, an agile absence on the air.
I cannot say what, or why, or even when it was.
I only know it happened, and I was there.

INTO THE INSTANT'S BLISS

Into the instant's bliss never came one soul
Whose soul was not possessed by Christ,
Even in the eons Christ was not.

And still: some who cry the name of Christ
Live more remote from love
Than some who cry to a void they cannot name.

—after Dante

THE PREACHER ADDRESSES THE SEMINARIANS

I tell you it's a bitch existence some Sundays
and it's no good pretending you don't have to pretend,

don't have to hitch up those gluefutured nags Hope and Help
and whip the sorry chariot of yourself

toward whatever hell your heaven is on days like these.
I tell you it takes some hunger heaven itself won't slake

to be so twitchingly intent on the pretty organist's pedaling,
so lizardly alert to the curvelessness of her choir robe.

Here it comes, brothers and sisters, the confession of sins,
hominy hominy, dipstick doxology, one more churchcurdled hymn

we don't so much sing as haunt: grounded altos, gear-grinding tenors,
two score and ten gently bewildered men lip-synching along.

You're up, Pastor. Bring on the unthunder. Some trickle-piss tangent
to reality. Some bit of the Gospel grueling out of you.

I tell you sometimes mercy means nothing
but release from this homiletic hologram, a little fleshstep

sideways, as it were, setting passion on autopilot (as if it weren't!)
to gaze out in peace at your peaceless parishioners:

boozeglazes and facelifts, bad mortgages, bored marriages,
a masonry of faces at once specific and generic,

and here and there that rapt famished look that leaps
from person to person, year to year, like a holy flu.

All these little crevices into which you've crawled
like a chubby plumber with useless tools:

Here, have a verse for your wife's death.
Here, have a death for your life's curse.

I tell you some Sundays even the children's sermon
—maybe especially this—sharks your gut

like a bite of tin some beer-guzzling goat
either drunkenly or mistakenly decides to sample.

I know what you're thinking. Christ's in this.
He'll get to it, the old cunner, somewhere somehow

there's the miracle meat, the aurora borealis blood,
every last atom compacted to a grave

and the one thing that every man must lose to save.
Well, friends, I'm here to tell you two things today.

First, though this is not, for me, one of those bilious abrading days,
though in fact I stand before you in a rage of faith

and have all good hope that you will all go help
untold souls back into their bodies,

ease the annihilating No above which they float,
the truth is our only savior is failure.

Which brings me to the second thing: that goat.
It was real. It is, as is usually the case, the displacement of agency

that is the lie. It was long ago, Mexico, my demon days:
It was a wager whose stakes I failed to appreciate.

He tottered. He flowered. He writhed time to a fraught quiet,
and kicked occasionally, and lay there twitching, watching me die.

SELF-PORTRAIT, WITH PREACHER, PAIN, AND SNOW

[John] Wheeler's delayed-choice experiment is a variation on the classic (but not classical) two-slit experiment, which demonstrates the schizophrenic nature of quantum phenomena . . . In the delayed-choice experiment, the experimenter decides whether to leave both slits open or to close one off *after the electrons have already passed through the barrier*—with the same results. The electrons seem to know in advance how the physicist will choose to observe them . . .

The electron . . . is neither a wave nor a particle. It is in some sense unreal; it exists in an indeterminate limbo. "Not until you start asking a question do you get something," Wheeler said. "The situation cannot declare itself until you've asked your question. But the asking of one question prevents and excludes the asking of another."

— JOHN HORGAN, *The End of Science*

Apart from and without Jesus Christ we can say nothing at all about God and man and their relationship one with another . . . We need to see that in view of God all our activity is in vain even in the best life; i.e., that of ourselves we are not in a position to apprehend the truth, to let God be God and our Lord. We need to renounce all attempts even to try to apprehend this truth. We need to be ready and resolved simply to let the truth be told us and therefore to be apprehended by it.

— KARL BARTH, *Church Dogmatics*

The eye with which I see God is the same eye with which God sees me.

— MEISTER ECKHART, *Sermons*

Stop warring with my God,
cried the dead woman

to her doctors, who believed
that speech, pulse, and pain

betrayed a life
they were yet meant to save.

So a rickety lift ascends
to a quick decline,

so a room assumes
one more degree of gone:

the love seat
like solid smoke,

the Goodwill card table
where she pasted

Easter seals and savored
preservatives, the weak tea

of Uptown dusk
seeping onto the cot

from which she's too tired to rise
when the new preacher stops by,

thumbing through psalms
and sympathies.

Stop warring with my God,
I told them,

she tells him,
who, a hectic hour later,

stops to look out the window
of the coffee shop

where he has been grappling
with nature and scripture,

God's absolute otherness
and electrons that seem to read

researchers' minds, the crux
at which to assert and to assent

become the same abrading verb.
She won't last the weekend,

he says, who said
to the woman whose sobs

fell soft as the late unstaying snow
that touching everywhere

leaves everything
even more bare:

The Lord is near to the brokenhearted
and saves the crushed in spirit.

For there is not a word in my tongue,
but lo, O Lord, thou knowest it altogether.

I shall be satisfied, when I awake,
with seeing your form.

THE RIVER

In the river where we've stopped something is moving, something is alive and writhing in the dark water toward me, in Africa, in the middle of the day. I can see the baked clay puzzling up the bank, the troubled shadows of the trees. I can see across the water two huge rocks sliding suddenly from the black mud, two pairs of eyes gliding against the stream. It is coming clearer. It is very hot. In the middle of the river drifting, in the current seething slowly closer, twenty of them, thirty of them: crocodiles feeding. I can see the stiff feet and the ripped flanks, the oils and the entrails, the pinkish, half-punctured gut of the small hippo bobbing in the water, slash and slash of red. I can see the weave and coil as if the water flexed itself, each welted crocodile taking turn, taking hold, swiveling from head to tail to tear the flesh and then the sudden satin of its open throat. So slow this current, almost imperceptible its tug. It's going to take a long time for this to pass, blood in the water, blood on the banks and in the leaves. It's going to take a long time before the gross bloat and wreck of the carcass curves out of sight, trees retrieve their shadows on the water, and my father, whom I have almost forgotten, breaks this silence.

THE SECRET

Daily higher the ivy dies,
Leaf by leaf subsiding white
Like a secret that seems to rise
Through vein and vine up to his eyes
And the green of what remains.
In spite of books and better light,
In spite of air and what friends say,
A rare arrested day, brief shoots,
In spite of all he cuts away:
From the ground up to the shelf,
From the leaves into the roots,
In spite of everything he tries,
Utterly the ivy tells itself.

WITNESS

Typically cryptic, God said three weasels
slipping electric over the rocks
one current conducting them up the tree
by the river in the woods of the country
into which I walked
away and away and away;
and a moon-blued, cloud-strewn night sky
like an X-ray
with here a mass and there a mass
and everywhere a mass;
and to the tune of a two-year-old
storm of atoms
elliptically, electrically alive—
I will love you in the summertime, Daddy.
I will love you . . . in the summertime.

Once in the west I lay down dying
to see something other than the dying stars
so singularly clear, so unassailably there,
they made me reach for something other.
I said I will not bow down again
to the numinous ruins.
I said I will not violate my silence with prayer.
I said *Lord, Lord*
in the speechless way of things
that bear years, and hard weather, and witness.

My quiet
Niagara

of unnameable
things

over again
I go

in my barrel
of prayer

HERE VISIBLE

Here visible
distance

is so much
a part

of things
things

acquire a kind
of space:

I reach
right through

the raking
tooth

that for so long
I've longed

to show you.
I touch

eternity
in your face.

ANTIQUITY TOO

Antiquity too
had arms, legs, loins,

and while its shadows thrashed on stone
it would one day be,

fucked, flicker-lit, like you, like me.

—*after Goethe*

AFTER A STORM

My sorrow's flower was so small a joy
It took a winter seeing to see it as such.
Numb, unsteady, stunned at all the evidence
Of winter's blind imperative to destroy,
I looked up, and saw the bare abundance
Of a tree whose every limb was lit and fraught with snow.
What I was seeing then I did not quite know
But knew that one mite more would have been too much.

COMING INTO THE KINGDOM

Coming into the kingdom
I was like a man grown old in banishment,
a creature of hearsay and habit, prayerless, porous, a survivor of
    myself.
Coming into the kingdom
I was like a man stealing into freedom when the tyrant dies,
if freedom is freedom where there are no eyes to obstruct it,
if the cold desert and the hard crossing were still regions of me.
I remember unremembered mountains, unspeakable weeds,
a million scents and sights I did not recognize
though they flowed through me like a land I inhabited long before
    belonging or belief.
Coming into the kingdom
I was like a man who imagines a city in flames and a city at peace
and sets out not knowing whether his homecoming
will be cause for sorrow or rejoicing,
or if indeed there will be one soul that knows him,
or if he is even the same assemblage of cells this side of exile,
or if exile is no longer what he once entered but what he is.
I tried to cry out in the old way
of thanksgiving, ritual lamentation, rockshriek of joy.
There was no answer. Had there ever been?
Remembering it now I do not remember
the arduous journey that must have rendered me a beast,
nor the broad gates opening at the last,
nor the children gathering around me in wonder,
nor the slow reclamation of a life I had been so long denied,
the million instants of exile told in tears.
Coming into the kingdom

I came into the damp and dirtlight of late November in north
    Chicago,
where the water-lunged bus chuffs and lumbers up Montrose,
and Butch's back gate's broken latch is impervious to curses,
and wires crisscross the alley like a random rune,
and an airplane splits and sutures the blue as it roars for elsewhere.

BETWEEN

Sometimes amid the starkrock
quality of sickness—

steel trays, sterile hands,
white walls like unlichened stone—

she felt, between herself
and her surround,

whatever rivers
through the nerves of birds

the moment before migration.

LITTLE RELIGION

His little religion
of common things
uncommonly loved
served him well.
Especially in hell.

*

When the sickbed sunlight
banishes shadows
like the noontime tin
of the storm cellar door
long, long before,
he is the blaze
it takes a man to raise,
he is the stone-
stepped dark a child
goes feelingly down.

*

As if to be
were to be
by oblivion
given
and forgiven
heaven.

VARIETIES OF QUIET

Varieties
of quiet

I quote
from a poet

no one knows.
And no one

knows
me too

if by chance
happening

here
some far year

when I am
not:

it matters
I tell you

it matters
the matter

one mind
collects,

one memory
protects

when memory's
kin

to that wordless
feeling

words
open in your head:

varieties
of quiet

varieties
of quiet

There are many
friend

as many
as the dead.

A POEM FOR EDWARD THOMAS

I never understood quite what was meant by God.
I never mastered that black bafflement
on which some seem to thrive as light.

To be sure, it's a shriveled soul
—it's a soulless shiver—
that in the self-delighting skywriting of swallows
discerns a curse both of and on the earth.

The meanness, the acidic blight in the veins,
that makes one hear even in a bird's
blind unbewildered strains
the grind of machine
creates, too, the compulsion to feed oneself to it.

Edward Thomas, if the end is an engine
eating miles and stiles in a growl of iron,
if hell is the El in which I bounce and balance
manically on my way to work,
stapled to people, sweating hate,
once—toxic, late—I saw a grace of sparks
struck from the tracks
blast every residual individual dark
from every face turned to see it
vanish instantly into the air,
so fair it touched the roar with silence.

THREE

MORE LIKE

THE STARS

I don't want to be alive anymore.
I don't want to be alive enough to want that.

One is not meant to turn on one's creator
with ferocity expendable in only one way.

Or is that exactly how one is meant to turn
to burn

beyond the love that from beyond being
has come to us:

Christ's ever unhearable
and thus always too bearable
scream.

In love and dread we learn to listen
for beloved dread

coming upon us like a whiplash rain
we watch through a window.

In pain we learn pain.

Sometimes amid the rancid moonlight and mindlice of my insomnia
there gleams a scalpel blade

so clean with meaning
so shaped and sharpened to interstellar blue

that drawing it—in season due—
across my own throat

there comes not blood but an ancient answering
starlight.

Once upon a time in a pleasingly modern slaughterhospice
with a view of sky-contempted skyscrapers

and Lake Michigan's immaculate sewage
my inner skin was skinned mouth to bowels,

my soul—deadword, die to find it.

For self-pity there must remain a self.
Ah, but even shitting one's self

one still finds one's self hastening to hide it all
from the kind Ukranian nearly bearded night nurse.

Fentanyl patches patching my stalactite thighs
my diaphanous shoulders

the very air eating me
like a late leaf

that once I would have flourished
for a perishable lover

or lonelied like some catpiss poignancy
into a poem.

Dead brain, living will, little pills
entangling pain with adoration of it,

morphine machine whose little beep
(heavenly bell)

conjures me to the suddenly more tolerable hallways
of hell . . .
        Lovely Leila,

so unsurgically curved,
disclosing as she leans to clean my lines

a bit of icelace undergarment like the very last trace
of a glacier.

The brain the brain the brain flickering electrically
in and out,

in,
      out—

not the mind in which I love
my wife

whose tightwound nightmind conjures Christ in diapers,
for instance, filthy infant, or later,

in a mist of adolescent bad weather,
bored of wood, dogdead Judea, squawk-box God,

some restless absurdity of earth, she says,
through which the rest of heaven can come.

Once upon a time I walked through the chemical glamour
of a night refinery

sparking dangerously without and within
for beside me under her underclothes

undulated an incarnation
of creation's finest failure:

moonskin to make a young man wince
coupled with stifling innocence.

Still, we managed.

And over the wrought-iron railing of the country club
to which neither of us could possibly belong,

in the moonskinned pool that seemed both to embody and imbibe
her, we improved.

And later, out on a green (to be sixteen!)
when the starshower I thought was mine

was mining me for sweat, muscle, memory
to make its own death

shine unceasingly inside of me,
even unto hell,
                we excelled.

Can it be that her last name was really Key?

So much life in this poem
so much salvageable and saving love

but it is I fear I swear I tear open
what heart I have left

to keep it from being
and beating and bearing down upon me

What rest in faith
wrested
        from grief

What truce
        with truth
in bowing
down

not to the ground
of being
        but simply
to the ground

Affliction flickers
distant
        now
like a structure
on fire
        Love's
reprieve
moves through me

like a breeze

But antlike
        existence
crawls all over me Lord

and I cry out
if you call
     this vise
quiet
     a cry
this riot
of needs and genes
an I

Feelingly
     among the
bones
     and nerves
of sounds
I make my scathing
way
     Failingly
in church
or in the parked
car
     before work
I try
     to pray

What might it mean
to surrender
     to the wonder
nothing
     means

Not to end
        with a little flourish
                of earth

Not to end

Love is the living heart of dread

Love I love you unto the very edge of being

Dead

Something in us suffering touches,
teaches first to find

little coves in our loves: blank nothings
wherein we are what we always were

     —blank nothings—

but changed or rearranged
as atoms
       in the random
           kingdom
               of things:

hand, we say, or *eye*, or *hair*,
as if to make ourselves—to stake ourselves—truly
there

Knowing now not to move in time
we are moved
          by tiger-striped tails
bloodfine fins

some natureless cerulean
one would say

thinking oneself
out of nature

Something in us, suffering, touches,
torches,
          so we may saunter
seeingly
through an altogether other

element,
as once in the Shedd Aquarium in Chicago

        I floated   a moment

with my love and the two new lives
borne from us
                who loved best
the eensy
          green
                  almost
                          unfish

more like the stars

when you close your eyes and whirl
open to the whirling

grains
so freed from things
                      you fall
                                down
                                      laughing

at the havoc

For me for a long time
not the minnows mattered

but the pattern after: miraculous
I didn't think

to think:
all those mite-eyes and animate instants

answering at once to my need
and to nothing

as if my very nerves worked
in finally a saving sense

Something in us touches
suffering
            touching
us

like the constellations
of kinetic quiet

that bound us beyond us
as right to the wall the girls pressed

their still-forming faces
through which the wild new schools flew
almost
too green
too blue
to stand

And I held your hand.

NOTES

ACKNOWLEDGMENTS

NOTES

"Wartime Train" derives from Sándor Csoóri's poem of the same title. It is not a translation or even a version but simply a poem that would not have existed without Csoóri's poem having paved the way. Similarly, "Antiquity Too" is the result of thinking about a late fragment from Goethe, which now I can't even track down for comparison. As someone once said: Immature artists imitate, mature artists forget.

"Into the Instant's Bliss" is a loose translation of lines 103–108 from Canto XIX of Dante's *Paradiso*:

> *A questo regno*
> *non salì mai chi non credette 'n Cristo,*
> *né pria né poi ch'el si chiavasse al legno.*
>
> *Ma vedi: molti gridan "Cristo, Cristo!",*
> *che saranno in giudicio assai men prope*
> *a lui, che tal che non conosce Cristo*

"Varieties of Quiet": The phrase comes from Larry Eigner.

"A Poem for Edward Thomas": The first line of this poem is from Thomas's war diary. The last line is from his poem "Ambition." The speaker is me.

ACKNOWLEDGMENTS

I am grateful to the editors of the following magazines, where versions of these poems first appeared: *The American Scholar, The Atlantic Monthly, Books and Culture, The Christian Century, Commonweal, The Cortland Review, Economy, The Hopkins Review, Image, The Nation, Negative Capability, The New Criterion, Poetry Ireland Review, The Rumpus, Slate, Spiritus, 32 Poems,* and *Tikkun.*

Also, many thanks to Ilya Kaminsky and Nate Klug, old friends with avid eyes.